To
Matt –
with best wishes
and God's blessings

Georg Rehloff

WHAT JESUS TAUGHT AND WHY IT MATTERS

Towards a Christianity With No Other Foundation But Christ

Georg Retzlaff

authorHOUSE®

AuthorHouse™
1663 Liberty Drive
Bloomington, IN 47403
www.authorhouse.com
Phone: 1-800-839-8640

First published by AuthorHouse 9/23/2010

ISBN: 978-1-4520-7719-2 (e)
ISBN: 978-1-4520-7718-5 (sc)

Library of Congress Control Number: 2010913415

Printed in the United States of America

This book is printed on acid-free paper.

Dedicated to the People
at
ASECC

with Faith, Hope, and Love,
These Three.

Table of Contents

THE GOOD NEWS
SEMINAR

INTRODUCTION

What has been masquerading as Christianity all these centuries would scarcely be recognized by the One who started it. A specter is haunting the Christian world: what if we had squandered two thousand years, claiming Him to be the "Lord" but setting up ourselves as ultimate authorities over what defines "Christianity"? Could it be possible that we wasted our lives by believing and proclaiming something that Jesus Himself would disown? Have we created Christian cultures, nations, civilizations which betray next to no kinship to the proclaimer of the Good News?

It is rather amazing that there seems to be no consensus among either clergy or laity as to what the Gospel is. After 2000 years: no clarity of purpose, preaching, practice! The end result: a faith so fragmented and shattered into many hundreds of denominations that its demise would be neither astonishing nor lamentable. Christianity, if it is not clear about the Good News of Jesus, does not deserve to exist. It is a travesty.

The Good News Seminar is the result of years of struggle in a parish whose mission statement is "Living and Sharing the Gospel of Jesus". It was our finding that the "living and sharing" wasn't working well because there was no "knowing" what the Gospel really is. Over many months, small groups of five men or five women, separated by gender, would meet, once, for three hours, and ponder the foundations of the Christian life. This is the Good News Seminar: a brief, radical look at what the Gospel is, and what it means to live accordingly.

Don't read on if you are happy, healthy, content with your life, your family, your work, yourself. This is a book for those in pain and turmoil, for the lapsed, the disenchanted and bored, for the valiant enemies of a faux Christianity who can't quite let go yet. Here may be your chance. Tolle, lege!

G.R.

PERSONAL STATEMENT

This book should have been written much earlier but it took a lifetime to see more clearly. After nearly four decades of ministry I feel compelled to examine my own preaching and ministry. What is success? A large parish? A huge budget? Many programs? Impressive facilities? None of that matters now, though it did once, in the halcyon days after ordination, when I subscribed to those notions. Now, what matters, are legacy, continuity, a congregation deeply rooted not in numbers or numbing activities, but in knowledge. A priest's work is not done when people offer him love and support but when they allow him to gently slip away, to a new assignment or into retirement. There will be no crisis, no "mourning", no soul searching, no surveys. They will know who they are, and what their task is. All ministry is interim ministry: in between, between the predecessor and the successor, between heaven and earth, between human nature and the born-again life. It must be the greatest joy of a priest when people no longer remember him but HIM to whom he bore witness.

PARISH SITUATION

It was probably never easy to be a genuine Christian community but today's problems are clearer than ever before. The following assessment will not fit every parish, anywhere, but many a parish, somewhere.

The global situation is characterized by a drift into generic religion, a diffuse spirituality, a kind of "world-faith", akin to world music or global economics. There is a continuum of competing forces, from gross superstition to secular humanism, which attract and abstract people who used to function within traditional parishes. The Gospel seems to be a still small voice compared with the din of religious globalism.

The national situation – and I am talking here of North America – is less and less conducive to a faith which, historically, is connected to the Old World, especially to Anglo-Saxon culture. Our ethnic situation, highly volatile and changing almost daily, favors a kind of multi-cultural mix which relegates traditional Christianity to a minor role.

The ecclesiastical situation seems precarious. Based on the two previous observations, mainline churches scramble to fit in, adjust, conform, and please. Gender and sexuality issues continue to cause huge rifts and schisms within established denominations, weakening their base, and exposing the "emperor without clothes".

The demographical situation in many communities reveal a parish's dependence on an accustomed constituency: ethnicity, color, social and economic status all contribute to a parish's self-image and identity. A changing environment often leaves a parish stranded either in the past, or as an island, surrounded by alien offshoots, visited by commuters from far away.

The parochial situation is often marked by fear and animosity: fear to address relevant issues because of their potential divisive nature, and old resentments, fault lines, party allegiances which prevent a coming together as disciples of Jesus. Sub-groups of the parish group tend to persist, in contradistinction of each other, even if there are just two or three gathered in their own name.

The religious situation is the most dismal. It is at the time of ministerial transition, from one leader to the next, that the truth will both come out into broad daylight and be smothered immediately under a mountain of expediencies, practicalities, and lowest common denominators. One treads on a carpet which is seriously warping with all the issues swept under it: the fact that there is no consensus on the Gospel, on what it means to be Christian, on what the purpose of the church is, how worship or Christian education should be done.

PROPOSED STEPS

The parish will die, indeed, it must and should die if it does not know its raison d'être. There ought to be a core of people who know the Gospel of Jesus Christ, and are capable of communicating this effectively in word and deed. The retired bishop of New York, the Rt. Rev'd Richard F. Grein once wrote, "Why are we not attracting new members? My thought is that it is because in large measure we are trying to draw people into a body of believers that is not clear about what it believes" (The Living Church, January 14, 2007, p. 15). This must change. The Good News Seminar is an attempt to gather people in small groups, five each, around one table, for a period of three hours. It seemed prudent to separate men from women to allow for free discussion, unencumbered by any extraneous influences. All seminars were identical: one hour was dedicated to debunking traditionally held ideas about Christianity; another was devoted to the Good News Jesus preached; the third dealt with the practical consequences of the Gospel in daily life.

POTENTIAL SIGNIFICANCE

I have undertaken this effort as an Episcopal priest in an Episcopal parish in the USA. However, I do believe that the Good News Seminar can be a useful tool beyond national and denominational boundaries. Christian people are pretty much the same anywhere. The Seminar is an offering of love to the church, the spotless bride of Christ and the harlot of Babylon. It may produce results. It may. It is not a tool to generate desired outcomes, it leaves room for grace. It knows human nature: some people will not hear at all; others will hear but not listen; a few will listen but won't understand; even fewer will understand but then are fearful to act upon their understanding. And then, there may be two or three who hear, listen, understand, act, and lead the church towards Him who is the Way, the Truth, and the Life.

INTRODUCTION
TO THE SEMINAR

So many parishes claim that they want to share the Gospel of Jesus Christ with the world. So far, so good. It is obvious that the church of Jesus must do that. The problem is only that there is no consensus on what constitutes the Gospel. This is rather mind-boggling: how can a religious faith endure if its adherents cannot even agree on what makes up its core?

In the following seminar I shall refer to scripture but must issue a caveat: others use scripture texts as well. Scripture does not "prove" anything. The truth is not found in a text, nor in a context, or subtext. Truth is an event when something becomes existentially relevant, when it hits you between the eyes, when it "speaks to my condition" (George Fox was right here). This is the place to humbly recognize that Bible texts can be useful but will never be cogent. A book of sixty-six volumes, spanning a millennium of writing and editing, will surely fail to provide proof. Others can and will prove other "gospels", seemingly equally authentic, by resorting to scriptural quotations. When I use text, it is only for one purpose: that I believe in a Text, a fabric of reason and faith, within the text; that not all Scripture is created equal; that the New Testament trumps the Old; the gospels rank higher than Paul; that the Synoptics are closer to Jesus (maybe) than John, and that the Sermon on the Mount is a pinnacle that leaves in the dust the secondary ruminations of gospel redactors. Therefore the Good News Seminar cannot be "right". It can only become right in the eyes of those who see. I have to abandon all attempts at scriptural proof-texting: it never worked in Christian history, and never will. It is my humble wish that what I propose is in accordance with the Word, as I embrace and cherish it. Biblical theology is an oxymoron: one can never cast a grid of coherence and logic over a book that served peoples in many countries, over many centuries, written in three different languages, appealing to, and reflective of, vastly diverging cultures. So, when I quote scripture, it is with a spirit of recognition, of familiarity, of friendship. I am aware that there are other texts which "contradict" my readings. I acknowledge that there are scholars whose readings differ from mine. None of that matters. Buried under the scriptural mountain is the precious pearl of great price. To unearth, shine, and present it to the world is our task. That many will disagree can be expected but I shall meet them not on the battle field of noisy textual swordplay but in the still, small chamber of conscience: does it make sense to be a Christian, and if so, why?

The Good News Seminar's principles are simple: "Good News" is the modern translation of "Gospel", which derives from "Godspell", literally the "spelling out of good news". We are concentrating here on the Gospel preached by Jesus: what HE said was Good News. His message was brief, new (which means: upsetting the known and accepted doctrine) and simple.

Misunderstanding
the Gospel

The biggest obstacle to learning is knowing. All learning is displacing and eradicating what has been planted in the brain. Jesus was called "Teacher" most of the time, His followers were disciples, the Greek work for which means "students", "learners". "News" cannot be received until "olds" has been discarded. If the Gospel is indeed "euangelion", i.e. good news, it will ask for, and demand, displacement of hitherto held beliefs. This was as painful then as it is now: to let go of the cherished assumptions about the Christian religion, things so familiar and close to us that they almost succeeded in overpowering the message entrusted to us.

BEFORE JESUS' TIME

The gospel of Jesus is brief, to the point, succinct. HE did not set up schools, devise curricula, or spend much time in any location. Mark 1:38-39 *And he said to them, "Let us go on to the next towns, that I may preach there also; for that is why I came out." And he went throughout all Galilee, preaching in their synagogues...*There was an urgency and brevity about His gospel that seems to elude our modern imagination which is absorbed in lengthy and tedious theological discourse. Gospel cannot mean a regurgitation of the Hebrew Scriptures. All the stories about Adam and Eve, about Noah, Abraham and Sarah, Isaak, about Moses, the law and the prophets may be interesting but they are <u>not</u> gospel. It is time for the Christian Church to realize that these narratives belong properly to our Jewish brethren; that Paul was right when he insisted that the way to Christ didn't have to go through hundreds of years and pages of Jewish lore. It is rather disheartening to see how Christians battle over issues of creationism vs. intelligent design (or worse: whether there were dinosaurs in Paradise!); the nature of women vis à vis men; the role of law within a religion of grace. All of these issues are irrelevant. Jesus did not come to reiterate the long story of God with one people but to point out the vision of a God for all people. In the famous Antitheses of the gospel according to St. Matthew, Jesus says, again and again, *It has been said to you from of old....but I say unto you..* What is old is not new, what is long cannot be brief. The Gospel of Jesus is not found in the pages of the old book, it's a new book in its own right. We need to let go (see part II of this book, Let My People Go).

At Jesus' Time

We can only understand the Gospel if we grasp the magnitude of the cross. What Jesus said was dangerous. His words created an unholy alliance of enemies from many quarters: Pharisees, Sadducees, Herodians, Romans, members of John the Baptist's movement, the mob. One does not get killed for repeating what was widely accepted anyway. Many of the traditional "Christian" beliefs now fall by the wayside. Jesus obviously was a friend of the Pharisees, he talked and ate with them, he shared their ideas about angels and guardian angels (Mt 18:10), about the resurrection (Mt 22:29-32), about Judgment Day, heaven and hell, the devil, about retributive justice. All of these ideas were common currency in the Judaism of Jesus' days, having been "imported" from Zoroastrianism in the 2nd century BC against the vehement opposition of the guardians of traditional religion, the Sadducees. None of these topics belong to Christianity proper . They do not threaten anyone. To preach on any of these topics would be tantamount to carrying coals to Newcastle. This cannot be the gospel. One does not get crucified for stating the received and popular version of religion. No one got killed in Israel for preaching about angels, eternal life, resurrection, heaven and hell.

That Jesus healed the sick and cast out demons could not have been it, either. Others did the same, with varying success (Lk 11:19; Mk 9:38; Acts 19:13ff). The gospel cannot be about getting health, food, or any other benefits. Jesus resisted these temptations early on (Mt 4). The healing of body and mind is a concern of religion in general, it is not a Christian preserve.

The greatest misunderstandings revolve around Jesus' "summaries" of the Law. Most Christians presume that the essence of the gospel is enshrined in the so-called Golden Rule. But this "rule" is neither Christian (Kung Fu Tzu, some 600 years before Jesus, formulated the same idea, sometimes referred to as "Silver Rule" because it uses the negative formulation, *don't do unto others what you don't want them to do unto you*) nor radical enough to warrant the cross. In fact, this "rule" simply sums up the old religion: *So whatever you wish that men would do to you, do so to them; for this is the law and the prophets* (Mt 7:12). No one would have ever been delivered to the Roman authorities for stating the obvious, eternally valid ethical principle of reciprocity. Immanuel Kant, 1700 years later, rephrased the Golden Rule in his "categorical imperative", and died peacefully after a long life in academia.

This leaves us with the Great Commandment, Mt 22:24-40: *But when the Pharisees heard that he had silenced the Sadducees, they came together. And one of them, a lawyer, asked him a question, to test him. "Teacher, which is the great commandment in the law?" And he said to him, "You shall love the Lord your God with all your heart, and with all your soul, and with all your mind. This is the great and first commandment. And a second is like it, You shall love your neighbor as yourself. On these two commandments depend all the law and the prophets."*

Repeated Sunday after Sunday, at the opening of the weekly Eucharist, this text has become the embodiment of what the Gospel stands for: love of God and neighbor. That Jesus' answer has next to nothing to do with genuine Christianity is lost on most, if not all people. A scribe asks Jesus to summarize the Old Testament law. Jesus replies with two quotes from that law: Deuteronomy 6:5 and Leviticus 19:18, doing just what the questioner had wanted: summarize the law. These rule-of-thumb pronouncements were neither original nor dangerous, they were popular with people who couldn't find their way around the bewildering multitude of ever-increasing regulations. No one, ever, in all of human history, had himself killed for stating the obvious, the pleasant, the easy and convenient: love God and neighbor, and you are OK! How could Christianity have ever slid down this slippery slope? The vast majority of people on earth, in one way or another, love "God" (some ultimate value) and strive to be nice. Volunteerism, charitable works, care for the needy: that's human or humanistic. Much great work is done by atheists and agnostics. If that's what Jesus came to proclaim as Good News, we need to look for a new religion! You don't sacrifice your life for the trite, the trivial, the undisputed. No, this is not the gospel of Jesus.

AFTER JESUS' TIME

The gospel of Jesus quickly turned into a gospel about Him, a convenient way to render Him irrelevant. The theological spin doctors went to work, probably even during His lifetime, to defang His true gospel by turning it into a message about Him. Now He did not have Good News, but He was Good News! It is one of the most tragic events in Christian history that those entrusted with His life-giving words turned into willing, second-generation executioners. They began speculating about His birth, His origin, His pre-existence, the so-called mysteries of the incarnation, the Virgin birth, the cosmic effect of the salvific cross, the resurrection, ascension, His return, the end of time, the role of the Holy Spirit in all of this. A witch's cauldron was heated up to cook a Gospel soup which unsuspecting eaters still slurp, Sunday after Sunday, believing it to be the real thing. What people said about Jesus, during His lifetime and after, cannot possibly constitute the Gospel He preached, for which he suffered and died. The doctrines about Jesus, however justified they may be, cannot, and must not, be a substitute for the gospel. They are too complicated. We know why and when they came about. In Palestine, Jews (for Jesus) tried to justify to Jews (against Jesus) why they continued to follow Him as their Messiah. They enlisted the help of prophets and psalmists to concoct a mélange of texts purporting to make Him into someone who would "fit" into a scriptural straight-jacket. They largely ignored Him, the Word. They spoke about Him, in their words. Paul and others, desperate for effective mission in the Gentile world, created a vocabulary suited for Greeks and their infatuation with philosophy. In both cases, the real Jesus and His gospel were sacrificed: here on the altars of traditional religion and there in the interest of successful expansion. We are still looking for the real gospel, the Words of Eternal Life!

UNDERSTANDING
THE GOSPEL

Good News cannot be received unless there is Bad News first. This is the particular problem of the church: it attempts to preach Good News to those who think they are good, feel good, think good about themselves already. But there is no Good News for those who neither expect nor need any. Bumper stickers reading "Christ is the Answer" don't mean much unless, and until we talk about the question, the quest, the underlying problem. We need to talk about the human condition, about misery, sickness, evil, suffering, injustice, oppression, poverty, death. "Jesus" doesn't mean anything much to people who are well-adjusted, content, young, beautiful, and strong. He doesn't mean anything to people who do not think, wrestle, struggle, deal with mega-problems of relationships, careers, sexuality, identity, existential doubts. It's like throwing your "pearls before swine" if the church attempts to preach the Gospel to those who are not in despair. They are out there: the ones on the edge, those who question, wonder, weep, and yearn for change; change in themselves, the world, in others, in everything. The Gospel is for them. No one else will get it, no one else is ready. There is no answer for those who do not question. There is no Good News for those who do not suffer from Bad News.

TRADITIONAL ANSWERS

The Hebrew Scriptures present the idea of the Kingdom of God (or Heaven) as the panacea for human misery: a vision of a peaceful, beautiful world in which there is no more crying, no more hunger or pain. When Jesus preached about the Kingdom of God (His only topic of importance!) He was aware of the fact that people had preconceived ideas. He preached as much <u>the</u> kingdom as <u>against</u> it. There were at least four distinct ideas of the perfect world, the Kingdom of God, prevalent in His days. We cannot understand the Cross unless we grasp the magnitude of His proclamation of Good News, a radical departure from all known and well-understood models of happiness. The Good News of Jesus' Kingdom contravened all known models, refuted them, proved them to be absurd, misleading, and spiritually harmful. Let's look at them.

GOD

One traditional expectation was that God would, one day, step in, correct all errors, bring about a brave new world under His most gracious rule. The key text for this expectation seems to be Daniel, chapter 7. Here we meet the "Son of Man", a rather elusive figure, whose identity cannot be made out with certainty. He stands next to the throne of the "Ancient of Days" (God), seems to act on His behalf, is sent down to earth to "fix things" in a godly way. The Son of Man's preferred modus operandi was to cleanse the earth of evildoers, thereby creating a kind of heaven on earth. He would come with a heavenly army of angels, on clouds, announced by trumpet sounds, a great celestial spectacle for all to behold. They could look to the skies for signs. Soon, very soon, it would be happening! The great advocate for this Son of Man probably was John the Baptist who preached a firebrand kind of "gospel". The one he expected would "cut down trees without fruit", he would have a winnowing fork in his hand and separate wheat from chaff, and burn the chaff with inextinguishable fire (Mt 3). John believed in an extraterrestrial God who would step into this world and make it right by simply exterminating the sinners, while leaving the righteous behind. He must have thought that Jesus was this kind of man: righteous, radical, ruthless. After hearing reports of Jesus' fellowship with "sinners" he had second thoughts, *"Are you he who is to come, or shall we look for another?"* (Mt 11:3) This may well have been the point of departure between the Baptist and Jesus who, otherwise, may have been, at some time, very close to each other. Jesus ate with sinners, forgave them, redefined what sin really is (potential, not action, Mt 5), and never believed that wiping out sinners would solve the problem of sin. Jesus was not the "Son of Man". His gospel mission was neither coercive nor punitive, but invitational and persuasive. The "Son of Man's" kingdom was the kingdom of a graveyard, not the wide open prairie of conversation and conversion. The God of the Hebrew Scriptures had made this mistake many times before: killing those who stood in His way did not solve the problems of the human race. By seeking the company of "sinners" Jesus rejected the first of the four known models of the Kingdom. He began to make enemies.

GOVERNMENT

People do not ever give up hope that one day, from among them, a leader would arise, a true Anointed One, an embodiment of divine justice and righteousness. The Israelites had their share of kings. They had been warned by Samuel (1 Samuel 8) but they did not relent: some king, at some time in the future, would be the right one, who would create a kingdom worthy of God's Name, God's kingdom. He would be the Good Shepherd (Ezekiel 34), a king like David, perfect (sort of) and just, he would guarantee economic equality, peace, and prosperity (Micah 4:3-4). This Anointed One (or, in Hebrew, Messiah, or, in Greek, Christ) would have the right programs in place to rid the world of evil, oppression, and poverty.

At Jesus' time, there were many who were looking for the Messiah. Then, as now, anyone able to feed multitudes, to dispense health care for body and mind (for free!) would have mass appeal. That Jesus has felt the temptation to be the Messiah is beyond doubt. He had power, it emanated from Him, those who touched Him felt it. It is no surprise that those who were fed and healed wanted to make Him king (royal highness, Messiah) by force. He withdrew (John 6:14-15), he resisted. He could have agreed to, but didn't restore the glory of Israel (Luke 24:21), did not lead a political movement to change the situation of people on earth (John 18:36 My kingship is not of this world). It must have felt like a slap in the face when the long-expected Christ/Messiah rode into Jerusalem on a donkey, not a horse; His followers waving palm branches, not brandishing swords; their lips not shouting martial tunes but pouring forth Hosannas! It was Jesus' last (and unsuccessful!) attempt to let people know: I am not the king you expect, I came not to change the system but the heart. The messianic, Christian Jesus is a political figure whose charisma would bring about ephemeral change, peripheral improvements, but no rebirth, no new beginning. By avoiding the political aspects of the Kingdom Jesus rejected the second of the four known models of the Kingdom. He continued to make enemies.

GROUP

There were people with whom Jesus connected, for whom He felt a certain kinship: those who wanted to excel, who strove for perfection, who believed earnestly in the possibility of a New Life in this life. The Pharisees were His friends. He ate with them; they warned Him of impending danger (Luke 13:31); He shared their views on resurrection, angels, the Spirit, Judgment Day, heaven and hell: all rather traditional and common ideas at the time Jesus grew up. That His erstwhile friends turned into His fiercest enemies must give us cause for thought. The Pharisees' Kingdom of God was a club, so to speak, an association of people with a special and supererogatory dedication. The very name of "Pharisee" possibly spells "separation", "apartheid" in Hebrew. Theirs was a rather simple and understandable world view: there are good and evil people in this world; the good must unite to exclude and defeat the evil by intensified piety, extra works of mercy, more and public prayers, and above all: disassociation from all those who don't agree with this rigorous program. The Pharisees were "good people" relating to other good people, creating the Kingdom among themselves by way of exclusion. Theirs was a black-and-white view of the world: God punishes sinners and rewards the righteous, therefore we will separate ourselves from sinners and consort with the righteous. The converse was also true for them: if you were obviously "punished" (sick, poor, down and out) you must have done something to deserve it. Or: if you were healthy, wealthy, and happy, God's stamp of approval on your life was obvious. Too bad: Jesus ate with sinners and outcasts, forgave them; extended His hand to Romans, Syrophoenicians, Samaritans, women, and children. His kingdom was not the kingdom of the Pharisees. Nor was it that of the Essenes, that group of people who, disenchanted with the way things were going in Jerusalem, fled to their desert monasteries at the Dead Sea, literally a "Dead" Sea: really holy people, totally segregated from the masses, they believed the Kingdom would come, very soon, to them!

We still have not overcome this approach to the Kingdom, there are still, out there, Christian groups who separate themselves from society. They are the "chosen ones", the children of God who would not be defiled by contact with the wicked world. They have erected fences, built walls, drawn lines of demarcation: there is an in-group and an out-group; there are the Amish and the English, the saved and the lost; the ones who belong to the only true religion and those who err, whether they be Roman Catholics, Baptists, Mormons, or Jehovah's Witnesses.

The Kingdom of Jesus is not here. If it's not for all, it's not for anyone. No one is good but God alone. We are in this boat together. No one can bail out. All those who withdraw from society to associate with like-minded perfectionists will find out, sooner or later, that, what they took with them from the "world" was their "selves", enough residue to make life behind the safe walls as much of a hell as the lives they left behind. The Jesus Kingdom is inclusive, gives hope to everyone, disparages all haughtiness and spiritual arrogance. By associating with non-Pharisees Jesus denounced the third of the four known models of the Kingdom. Here he made his most serious enemies.

GRAVE

This now is the Kingdom solution most familiar to us: perfect peace, justice, happiness will only be attainable in the next life. It is helpful to recall that the Hebrew Scriptures do not offer a conclusive solution to the problem of evil. The traditional system had God reward the righteous and punish the wicked in this life. There was no life after death according to the doctrine of the Sadducees. The book of Job gives us a fine example of the dilemma when "bad things happen to good people" (and vice versa). The "solution" was obviously found during the terrors of the second century BC, especially when

Antiochus IV Epiphanes was in power. Rising up against this ruthless Gentile ruler cost the lives of countless young men and brought the question to the fore: can injustice, cruelty, and wickedness triumph? Can God be just? In the face of the stark reality of the day a crutch was borrowed from the ancient religion of Zoroastrianism. What looks unfair now, will not be so for ever. There is a life after death, a Day of Reckoning, a turning of tables, judgment. Bad people may fare well in this life but will receive their deserved punishment in the next. Those who suffer now will enter Paradise. Thus the moral cosmic order will be maintained. Now the earth, this life, becomes the proverbial "vale of tears", a prelude to eternal happiness, a testing ground. It is probable that Jesus subscribed to that new-fangled philosophy, espoused by the Pharisaic Party to which He was very close early in His ministry. It must have been a popular kind of doctrine, solving all sorts of problems, giving hope and comfort to the distressed.

But this cannot have been the Good News, simply because it was "old" news. Not only was it an import from an alien religion, rightfully denounced as heresy by the stalwart defenders of the Biblical faith, the Sadducees, but it was also blatantly escapist, a doctrine for losers, the eternally resentful, the dreamers of vengeance, of hellish fires for their enemies, of unutterable joys for themselves, the righteous. By disappointing the other-worldly advocates of the Kingdom Jesus rejected the last of the four known models of the Kingdom. He had succeeded to make enemies of all.

Jesus' message of the Kingdom of God was fully understood by those who listened to Him (quite contrary to today's audience!). People had a clear concept of what He was talking about, they knew about the Kingdom. The cross on Calvary can best be understood when we grasp the depth of disappointment people must have felt when the one on whom they had pinned their hopes demolished their most cherished ideas: the Kingdom, if it is to come, will not be God's doing; no government can be perfect enough to usher it in; no association of righteous people will embody it, and forget about heaven! We need to hear what Jesus had to say, anew, afresh, unencumbered by historical ballast (see part III of this book).

The Answer

The oldest gospel, the first words Jesus spoke: *The time is fulfilled, and the kingdom of God is at hand; repent, and believe in the gospel.* (Mark 1:15). In today's language: rethink (the Greek metanoia does not mean repentance – feeling sorry for your sins – but change of mind!) your traditional ideas about the Kingdom and look at something entirely novel. Could what we have traditionally called the Kingdom be actually here, within reach, within us, among us (Luke 17:21)? The core of Jesus' teachings is not theological but anthropological. All four received Kingdom ideas expressed a yearning for deliverance from evil. All four located it "somewhere out there", comfortably tagged onto others: the devil, bad rulers, wicked people, the way things are in this world. Both liberating and threatening at the same time was the amazing notion that the "problem" lies within human nature: "*For from within, out of the heart of man, come evil thoughts, fornication, theft, murder, adultery, coveting, wickedness, deceit, licentiousness, envy, slander, pride, foolishness. All these evil things come from within, and they defile a man*" (Mark 7:21-23). According to Jesus, there are no good or bad people, just people who share the same predisposition, character, potential. The famous Antitheses in the Gospel of Matthew, chapter 5, point out the commonality of the human condition: not what we do matters (Jesus forgave the "doers" and ate with them!) but what we are all capable of. This shift from doing to being marks the center of the gospel of Jesus Christ. There is something about this "faithless and adulterous generation" (Luke 9:41) that is not limited to a "generation" but extends to the species itself. The human race is a troubled one. It came late, in the big evolutionary scheme of things, resting on, and benefiting from, the labor and sagacity of millions of other organisms, for billions of years. The appearance of man upon the scene has spelled doom and disaster for the world. It's the only species driven by discontent with itself, gifted with superior intelligence (or so it claims) and cursed with a unique myopia. It charges ahead without regard for consequences, has talent for development but is hampered by ignorance. In the words of Albert Schweitzer, "Man has lost the capacity to foresee and forestall. He will end by destroying the earth". The only critique here: did man lose it or never have it in the first place? Jesus seems to have had an insight that can resonate with us moderns: there is something wrong with us, not with bad people, but with people, period. It does not help to seek refuge in the Creation story and cite from the book of Genesis: let us make man in our image! Here is a god-like man, strutting about, subduing the earth, multiplying recklessly, eating everything in sight, including that which is "forbidden". That's not the man Jesus was, or talked about. Jesus looked at the human heart and saw what we all see, in those rare moments of grace when Truth happens within.

Human Nature

"Oversexed, Overfed, Over here": that's how Americans were viewed in Britain during WW II. Since Americans are humans, we have here an accurate assessment of human nature in general. Sex, greed, and power: they make us a species unique among all other living beings on this planet. It is a pleasant surprise to see that the Catechism in the Book of Common Prayer (An Outline of Faith) begins not with God, creation, the cross, but with the fundamental question, What are we by nature? (BCP, p. 845). Christianity must begin with anthropology, not theology, the thinking about man, not about God. In other words: the problem is not "out there" but "in here". If that's the case, then the solution is also not "out there" but "in here"! Where there is the problem there is also the solution: man is both.

The scientific method begins with problem awareness. No science can be done until, and unless we are aware of a "problem", an issue, of something that pricks our interest, curiosity. We need to go back again in detail to the one scriptural text which I deem foundational, Mark 13:30, a text that talks about the end times. Wars, earthquakes, famine, environmental changes, atmospheric phenomena are "predicted" here. And then comes verse 30: Truly, I say to you, this generation will not pass away before all these things take place. Long understood as a prediction of the impending end, soon to take place, within the lifespan of the hearers, this one sentence can serve as a wake-up call. The word "generation" seems to refer to the present, but the Greek word "genea" has a much wider meaning: human race, species, family of man (genealogy is the study of one's family throughout history!). "Pass away": the Greek "parelthē" can mean "pass away, go away, pass on". Here is my take: the present species, called human, will not rest until (mechris hou) all these things take place. My Jesus is not a predictor of future events but an analyst who opens my mind to see where I am. I am human. I am bent on self-destruction. I will, qua humanity, take down, with me, everything around me. Now I am listening. This sounds way too familiar, too true, too authentic. Could it be that Jesus, 2000 years ago, had a keen understanding of human nature that only now we moderns begin to grasp? That there is something within us that steers us towards oblivion? That there will be no hope, no life for us until we see, and see clearly? The world is going to hell in a hand basket, and it's us humans, not any other species, that stuff the basket. The signs are all around us, in fact, the signs are within us. Whatever disasters there are, they are not the concoctions of a warped divine mind, intent on inflicting unspeakable pain on His creation. The signs are OUR doing, because we can't help ourselves, we are, what we are, human. Let's have a look at human nature and its effects on life, on our future.

Sex

Look at the world of other living things: sex is procreational; sex is seasonal; sex is temporal. That's the way sex works: it is meant to produce offspring, there are times when it is most conducive, and there is the non-sexual life before and beyond estrus. There is fierce competition during the rut season, frantic activity while it lasts, but then calm begins its gracious reign. There are some species which, genetically, are unable to mate with more than one partner. Humans differ from other animals. Our sex drive is innate, life-long, expansive. We know no mating seasons, no estrus limitations, in fact, our nature seems to be sexual. No other species is capable of moving its primal instincts from procreation to recreation by artificial means of contraception, in vitro fertilization, artificial insemination, sterilization and surrogate motherhood. We like indiscriminate sex, all the time, with as many partners as possible, under all sorts of disguises. This is human. It is also the human tragedy. Far from being a gift from "God", it appears, at times, to be a curse from hell. One does not have to subscribe to the views of the Freudian school of psychology to see that our insatiable libido is the single-most powerful source of unhappiness, the driving force behind many of our thoughts, words, and deeds. The misery of puberty, the confusing signals of attraction, the loneliness, the search for futile satisfaction, the fear of impotence and undesirability: a huge industry has sprung up to "aid" us: Internet filth and its soft TV versions, pharmaceutical crutches to prop up a failing man- or womanhood. Proof enough to show: humans are relentlessly and recklessly sexual by nature, from cradle to grave, inside and outside of marriage. We need to see this as a problem, as in fact we begin to do when we look at AIDS (largely a heterosexual issue in most of the world); at STD among our teenagers (and also wildly promiscuous seniors!); at the break-down of families; divorce rates; domestic abuse; crime committed for sexual purposes: the list goes on. Unbridled, undisciplined sexuality is, at least, one of the causes of the population explosion, of friction between groups competing for resources such as water and food. And yet, the prevailing culture encourages and entices us to more and more sexual activity and awareness, glamorizing the lives of "sexy" people and their pursuits. Our education- and efficiency-driven world demands more and more years beyond sexual maturity to be devoted to career planning and development, stunting normal pro-creative sexuality into suppressed or recreational outlets which promise happiness. Fact is: there is no pot of gold at the end of that rainbow!

The church today is rather quiet on this issue, in fact, it seems to acquiesce. There are few, if any, sermons or teachings on human sexuality. That would be too embarrassing. People would object to being told what to do, or not to do, in the privacy of their bedrooms. Maybe the marriage ceremony is the last hold-out, when couples are asked to promise "to forsake all others". Here we catch a last glimpse of discipline, of problem-awareness, or religion's role in curtailing this aspect of human nature. From "be fruitful and multiply" and King Solomon's 700 wives and 300 concubines (1 Kings 11:3) to the polygamous adventures of Biblical personages there is only a short path to the "forbidden fruit" of Eden and the multitudinous laws attempting to govern run-away sexuality.

The Gospel is clear: what people do (harlotry, adultery, etc.) does not interest Jesus. He knows that this is human. He is more concerned about the potential than the action. He knows that normal men look at women "lustfully"; that the "eye is not sound". He has no problem with those "caught in the act". It is liberating to hear Him spell out where the problem is: in the human heart, the human condition, the human genetic code (Mk 7). Man has to transcend man to find happiness. Sin, for Jesus, is not the transgression of a commandment, but the living out of one's potential. It's not wicked people who sin but people, end of story. The answer is proffered in Matthew 19:12: "*For there are eunuchs who have been so from birth, and there are eunuchs who have been made eunuchs by men, and there are eunuchs who have made themselves eunuchs for the sake of the kingdom of heaven. He who is able to receive this, let him receive it.*" A "eunuch" sees women as "people", not as objects of desire. The Kingdom will happen when more and more people will become "eunuchs", looking at each other as fellow travelers, companions, as children of God. This goes as much against the grain of human nature as the injunction to "forsake all others". Can it be done? Could that be the challenge and task before us? Could that be a promise held out in front of our eyes: yes, you can?

GREED

It has long been observed that the number one topic of Jesus' teaching is not eternal life, the soul, life after death, or anything like that but money (and/or the love of possessions). Wealth had long been seen as a sign of God's approval, a blessing conferred on righteous people while, conversely, poverty was viewed as a kind of punishment for sin. Humans differ from animals who sometimes are infinitely smarter than us. They do not seem to hoard (squirrels excepted maybe), collect, heap up beyond their ability to control. They take what they need, and take again when another need arises. The birds of the air, the lilies of the field: they have more understanding than the glorious Solomon whose fabled riches (1 Kings 10) were the result of reckless plundering, extortion, and senseless taxation which resulted in the break-up of his kingdom (1 Kings 12:1-5). The idea that God gives to the righteous and withholds from sinners was turned on its head by Jacob who promised allegiance to God in exchange for "stuff", "Then Jacob made a vow, saying, *If God will be with me, and will keep me in this way that I go, and will give me bread to eat and clothing to wear, so that I come again to my father's house in peace, then the LORD shall be my God, and this stone, which I have set up for a pillar, shall be God's house; and of all that thou givest me I will give the tenth to thee.*" (Genesis 28:20-22). All this fell apart when Job questioned the righteousness of God who seemed to deprive the righteous and meet out indiscriminate favors to the seemingly undeserving.

Humans want, and then they want more. They lack the natural intelligence to let go when their needs are met. This is not the place to give a comprehensive overview of greed in the Christian Bible. May it suffice here to refer to Luke 12:16-21. "Fool!" Here is the proper description of a dyed-in-the-wool capitalist who cornered the grain market, created artificial shortages, and died in the process (of heart disease, over-eating, or as victim of the wrath of the hungry masses). We are born naked and naked we will leave this world. But between these perimeters we expend an enormous amount of energy to accumulate stuff. If we gain a little, we try to gain more. Once we have more, we desire most. That goal achieved, we'll go for mostest. Happiness means: having it all! This is the human tragedy that we don't know when to say when, that we are not genetically coded for sufficiency. What is more tragic: we continue to emulate the exploitative character of Joseph (Genesis 47:20) rather than listen to Jesus. Daily bread, that's all I need, that which is needful for a day; a treasure of spirituality which cannot be destroyed by moths or rust; a freedom from things that allows me to enter a narrow gate, a poverty which is chosen (poor in spirit) rather than suffered. Few people want to hear this, least of all in our society where "making it big" is a sign of well-being, of success, of God's blessings. We tend to look with pity on the multi-millionaire stock broker from New York who's had it, lets his hair grow, buys a Harley, and throws his former life away. Or we arrest people who throw money from a high-rise (as happened some years ago in Toronto) because they want no more. Could it be that our anxieties are caused by our greed? Could it be that we can learn to step out and away from all that and be free? Could it be that Christians arise in the midst of a wealth-idolizing "culture"? That their wealth is inside, hidden, shining like a precious pearl which overt wealth would only obscure? The foolishness of coveting as expressed in Mark 7:20-23 stands against the "greed is good" of "Wall Street" (both the place and the movie starring Michael Douglas). The Kingdom will happen when people wake up and see: having is easy, being is hard; accumulating is normal, letting go is special. The "Kingdom" happens when one person steps away from the brink of delusional happiness, in a municipality, a state, a parish, a diocese, when assets begin to be seen as liabilities. Can it be done? Could that be the challenge and task before us? Could that be a promise held out in front of our eyes: yes, you can?

POWER

Again, the question is: what makes us human? How do we differ from all other organisms on planet Earth? It seems that we not only do not have a natural, built-in mechanism for controlling our wants and our sex drive but are also incapable of reining in our desire to dominate others.

This is easily the scariest malfunction of humanity as it exists. We are driven by a lust for power which is both irrational and self-destructive. We love to impose our wills on others (it begins in the play pen!) and do not rest until we get to the top. We are not "wired" for synergy, gentleness, cooperation, peace. Everything in us screams survival of the fittest, scramble, step on and over others, use them, abuse them, if it gets us what we want.

The history of this "generation" of humans is rather unpleasant. Exploitation, war, suppression, torture, expansionism, empire-building, deprivation, curtailment of freedoms of others – on a smaller scale there is peer pressure, bullying, blackmail. Powerful people have the means to hire and fire, to build and destroy, to make and shake the fortunes of others. We stop at nothing. We don't know how to. Again, it's the paragon of the Old Man, Solomon, who can serve as a paradigm: the love of power lured him into reckless militarization, the acquisition of horses and chariots, the oppression of his own people (1 Kings 10). And all for the purpose of expanding his reach of power. Man, as he is, wants to gain the world and will lose his soul in the process (Mt 11:12). He will retaliate, an eye for an eye (Ex 21:23-25), or, worse, will inflict incremental damage on his real or perceived enemies (Genesis 4:23-24). There are no natural limits to the desires of man to control, dominate, or expand. It does not occur to man that there is no happiness at the end of this road. Maybe apart from cats, only man is capable of inflicting unspeakable suffering on other living things: the environment, plants, animals, and humans. We seem to be able to torture one day and go to church the next, to bomb a city filled with civilians now and receive a medal for that later. The human story is a tragedy of extension by all means. History teaches us nothing. The same mistakes will be made over and over again. We cannot detach ourselves from the illusion that power and violence guarantee permanency. There is no difference between democracies and dictatorships, monarchies and anarchies: they all are guided by humans whose goal it is to stay put by means of lording it over others: by war, by the penalty of death, by threats of dismissal, shunning, ostracization, destruction of reputation and career, by propaganda and brainwashing.

Is it possible to step away from the brink? Can "Good News" mean that there is an alternative to the innate drive toward crazy self-destruction? The gospel of Jesus offers the option of peace, of turning the other cheek, of not lording it over others, of an authority which is based on persuasion, not coercion. "Blessed are the peacemakers for they shall be called sons of God": what would the world look like if we, for just a moment, took our eyes off the "Son of God" (of creedal fame) and became "sons of God" ourselves? Became people who put the sword away, in the sure knowledge that those who take it will perish by it? That a life lived in total renunciation of any form of violence (verbal, physical, social) is infinitely more preferable to the scared existence of humans who trust in power?

Can it be done? Could that be the challenge and task before us? Could that be a promise held out in front of our eyes: yes, you can?

LIVING THE GOSPEL

JESUS

The gospel Jesus preached has been, and continues to be, rejected because we don't believe. We are too much a part of this world, too "realistic", too jaded to fall for fantasies. The "Kingdom" is a quaint, beloved notion but not one that can serve as a blueprint for a new humanity. We may have tried all or some aspects of it and found out: it just doesn't work because the "others" don't play along. So far we have focused on Jesus and His teachings. Now we need to turn our attention to His person. He lived His words, He was the Word. All our excuses and subterfuges won't work because of His life which presented to the world a new, unique unity of thought, word, and deed. The "Kingdom" is not a place, or a condition, or a hope: it's a life lived in trust and faith and conviction. In Him a new chapter of humanity was opened, here was a quantum leap, a bold and radical departure from a race that was doomed anyway.

The Gospels show us a Jesus surrounded by women who supported His ministry (Luke 8:1-3), who touched Him (Mark 5:27), spoke with Him in intimate privacy (John 4:27), let their hair down in front of Him (Luke 7:38ff), who were paraded in front of Him at the time of greatest vulnerability (John 8:1-11). Occasions of sin for any "normal" man. But here was more than "man": here was a new creation, a man who could look at a woman and see a child of God, not an object of desire, a person in need of being touched, not in body, but in soul. Let no man presume that it is impossible, that "boys will always be boys" (or girls will always be girls), that human nature is what it is, that nothing much will ever change. He did change all that. He lived His words. He was the Word, became a Word. The curse of relentless human sexuality was lifted in the life of the Holy One of God. He became the first of many brethren (Romans 8:29), instilling in us both hope and desire to become like Him, in life and death. Because He did it, it can be done. Once the precedent is established, recourse to old habits will no longer do. Man can move towards perfection, that is his call and only hope. It is significant that Jesus eschewed both the Scylla of gynomania (many wives, many children, much satisfaction) and the Charybdis of gynophobia (so characteristic of ascetic forms of religion). He did not steer the prudent via media, there is no whiff, here, of the Aristotelian Golden Mean. This is not compromise but a step forward. Here is a free man, free to look (without lust), to talk (without ulterior motive), to be touched (without taking it further). This is not human, this goes beyond humanity, onto a higher plain. This is where Kingdom people can gather.

JESUS AND POSSESSIONS

We need to mention that Jesus had money (Luke 8:1-3), in fact enough of it to appoint a treasurer for His movement, Judas Iscariot, enough not only to pay for His Band of Thirteen to move, eat, and sleep, but to give alms to the poor (John 12:4-6; 13:29). He presumably owned a house in Capernaum (Mark 2:1). He loved life, feasting, company to the extent that His detractors called Him a "glutton and a winebibber" (Mt 11:19). The "poor little Lord Jesus" is the invention of Biblically challenged people who often have little themselves and revel in resentment against those who do have. They feast on the "stable" in Bethlehem (quite a warm and comfortable place to dwell in given the alternative of a night out in the open) and the warning proffered to an all too enthusiastic follower that "the Son of Man has nowhere to lay his head" (Mt 8:20), a clear reference to Jesus' migrant, unsteady life which forced Him to change quarters frequently to avoid premature arrest. The despisers of this world have a hard time to claim Jesus as their own. He came, not to die, but to live and preach (Mark 1:38), and to live and preach well. Again, He did not steer the middle course, embrace the lukewarm compromise, the "both-and". In His attitude toward possessions He was free, almost to the point of recklessness. He had, and He didn't have; he gave away what others had given away. He saw how people were obsessed with wealth and goods and outward signs of God's approval on their lives – and parted company with them. His was not the choice between being a pauper or a potentate. He proclaimed and lived freedom, the ultimate dream of people who spend their lives on accumulating stuff only to discover that what they now control actually controls them. There is neither the embrace of the old ideology that God blesses, with material goods, those who play by the book, nor is there an ascetic world-denying disgust. His is a life filled with beauty and joy, day by day, where thanks is given for the bread (and the wine) that is needful for a day, where concerns about tomorrow are disregarded, where food, drink, clothes, and shelter are gifts from God who lets the sun rise, the rain fall, who makes lilies beautiful and fills the stomachs of hungry birds. The poor are lucky because they are free. The rich are unhappy because they are worried (Luke 12:16-21). Beyond infatuation and beyond renunciation there is the Jesus Way: the vision of a new man who gratefully receives, gracefully shares, and walks gently on the earth.

This is not human, this goes beyond humanity, onto a higher plain. This is where Kingdom people can gather.

Jesus and Power

Jesus was not a willing martyr. He knew enough about human nature to expect a violent response to His new vision of humanity. He, whenever possible, avoided conflict, ran away or hid Himself (John 6;15; 10:39; Luke 4:30). He had "safe houses" in which to spend the night. He clearly saw the curse on human nature which seems to condemn us to lust for power and domination over other by any means possible. He welcomed children, the most defenseless of all (Mt 19:14; Mk 10:14), frowned at His disciples' preoccupation with positions of power (Lk 9:51-55). He realized that coercion is not what changes human nature: threats and swords may cause the body to tremble, but the soul remains steadfast. Put your sword away, turn the other cheek, do not give an enemy the satisfaction of having brought you down to his level: love him, pray for him, be a servant. If it works, you have made a friend, if it doesn't you have not debased yourself. His kingdom is not of this world. If it were, His disciples would fight (John 18:36), but they didn't. The New Man, the Holy One of God He was, would not stoop to the methods of the Old Man. Even those who rejected Him, He refused to condemn or exclude (Mt 13:30; Mk 10:17-22).

That does not mean that He was a "doormat". He engaged His detractors in debates, arguing, with and without the use of Scripture; He cracked the whip to liberate the caged animals doomed to serve as sacrifices for human failings; He had fits of anger (Mk 3:5) and indignation (Mk 7:27). But we see in His life a steady progression towards wisdom (Lk 2:52). One cannot win anyone over by means of violence, threats, or coercion. The New Man used persuasion, compassion, gentleness, forgiveness. He invited, asked, taught. It was a life-long struggle, not a divine Given. He had to work this out: to offer His human Self in order to gain the Divine Self. To die alone, a shameful death, on the cross, and refusing to call on God to send an army of angels to end this all (Mt 26:53), this is the victory, it is finished.

This is not human, this goes beyond humanity, onto a higher plain. This is where Kingdom people can gather.

AND THIS IS THE GOOD NEWS:

We believe that those who know about, and suffer from their human nature can, by the Grace of God, be redeemed from mere humanity and enter a new state of being;

We believe that Jesus, through His words and life, defeated in Himself and others the forces of darkness and despair;

We believe that God's Holy Spirit, at work in a true Gospel Church, does nourish and strengthen those who dare to accept the gift of salvation from their old selves and become a new creation, at peace and in harmony with themselves, God, and the world.

CHURCH

Christians of the future will take Jesus seriously, begin to renounce the indoctrination of the past, and become simple disciples again. They will crave the abundant life in the Here and Now. They will understand that disciples are "learners". They will go through the pain of "unlearning" what has clogged their minds. They will find out that there is no Christian Ethics at all: no rules, no commandments, no paragraphs which, if followed, will guarantee a place in heaven, or, if contravened, will assure a place in hell. They have come to know Jesus as the eternal, loving, invitational voice of God's wisdom. Once they listen, they begin to struggle, just the way He did, with the newness of it all. They experiment, rejoice at progress, be baffled by back-sliding, but they will be steadfast on the path of the Redeemer. They embrace the promise of perfection, step by step, not as a means of an improved humanity but as its end. They cease to be humans and enter the realm He called the Kingdom of God, as beginners, as children, as forgiven sinners, as new creations, as Christians. They can now look at their lives not as realists but as believers: the Mustard Seed will grow! Out of the struggle come little victories: they have eyes to see that wealth is not the way to happiness (Mt 19:25); that lust for more sex is an illusion (Mt 19:10); that wielding the sword does not end but begets violence (John 18:10). They now shudder at the thought of the old humanity and wonder: how was it ever possible that we believed that this is all there is to man?

The end result is not a new law but a new species: horrified at the brutal excesses of capitalism with its never-ending desire for more; the silly dreams of world-domination by power and militarism which only create more hatred and resentment; the foolish temptation of hedonism which leads towards self- and other-destruction. Those in whom Christ has taken shape will be gladly poor, makers of peace, and pure in heart.

Nobody told them. Nobody threatened them. Nobody will reward them. They are what they are: the Body of Christ, a new Creation.

Practical Christianity

The church of the future will continue to baptize, solemnize marriages, and bury the dead. Christmas, Easter, and Pentecost will still be major holidays. But none of that will be of significance compared with its real purpose: to be a gathering place for learners (disciples) and sufferers.

Christians and Sex

The real Christian Church brings together the few who are honest about their experience of sexuality. They, as a community, pledge to keep the eye as light of the body. They dress modestly, without ostentation. They raise their children accordingly. They are on guard against the onslaught of TV, movies, the Internet, and what poses as "music" these days. They will not be guilt-ridden when they stumble, but fix their eyes on Him who blessed the pure of heart. They will not be judgmental but supportive of those whose failings become evident. They encourage discussing all issues of human sexuality openly and on all levels of Christian education. They will create a community of strong faith and forgiveness.

CHRISTIANS AND GREED

The church of the future is a small community welcoming those who struggle with wealth-addiction. It will neither condone nor condemn but counsel. This church does not raise funds but lives by faith. It needs not to tithe: neither to the parish, nor to the diocese, nor to the National Church. It wants the least from its members so they can make the least. They will, in teaching and practice, promote ways of simple living, individually, as a church, and as a nation. They are united in rejecting the culture of greed by teaching their children the difference between having and being. "To be better off" will now mean more peace, more freedom, more time. They will radically question the idol of Capitalism.

CHRISTIANS AND POWER

The gospel church will be a haven for those who "put away the sword" where conscientious objection is promoted, where war as a means to solve world problems is no longer accepted. Here people gather to commit to a bonfire the toy guns and other martial tools in the possession of their children. This church supports and encourages those who, because they will not register for the Selective Service, face discrimination. They will begin to look at abortion, capital punishment, and the wars of the past and present through the eyes of Jesus, the Prince of Peace. They have separated themselves from the culture of imperial militarism and refrain from glorifying warriors as heroes. Here are people who promote the Peace Corps, not the Marine Corps, who wrestle with issues of power and control, in politics, family, our neighborhoods, by offering true Gospel alternatives.

The Church of Jesus, no doubt, is a congregation of outcasts, they, the servants, are not above their Master. They will offer the world a better way: a way of Life. Because this is costly they will need one another for support, prayer, comfort. No one challenging the Powers That Be will go unharmed. The Empire will strike back. But the gates of hell shall not prevail against it: the Gospel is the last and only Good News, and, by the Grace of God, we shall know, live, and proclaim it.

LET MY PEOPLE GO

An Essay on the need for peace
between Christians and Jews

Anti-Jewish sentiments are probably as ancient as the Jews themselves. A highly intelligent, entrepreneurial people, successful in resource allocation, and gifted with superior skills does not have to wait long to be envied and despised. Be it the Egyptians (Psalm 105:25) or the Romans (Acts 18:2), Jews were under pressure to either assimilate or get out. We are not concerned here about the pre-Christian era, though. Whatever damage was done there, on either side, is not our concern. What matters to us is the Christian contribution to what is commonly called Anti-Semitism (preferably termed Anti-Judaism – since there are many other Semites, most notably Arabs, who do not meet with the same hostility). The purpose of this essay is to advocate a "velvet divorce", to recognize that Judaism is a religion that deserves to be respected in its own right, without doubling as a "precursor" to Christianity. As will be shown: both religions can benefit from a gentle and peaceful détente. In the end, Christians will understand that they will neither need nor deserve the "Old Testament"; Jews will see that their Holy Book is no longer hijacked by Christ-crazed fanatics who will stop short of nothing to interpret the Hebrew Bible according to their own whim.

Christians traditionally love the "Old Testament": it provides them with a cosmogony (the Creation Stories: yes, stories, there are two of them!), Adam and Eve, Cain and Abel, Noah, the Flood, the Tower of Babel. What would Sunday School look like without this treasure trove of stories? Of course: early Christianity had no Bible except the Hebrew one. Ironically, the history of Christian Anti-Judaism began as a conflict within Judaism. Those Jews who followed Jesus of Nazareth had to face their family members who were not. Often it was a matter of life and death (John 19:20), the fear of showing up on the radar-screen of the Roman Security Forces. One can easily imagine the heated discussions within the one and same Jewish family: I am right in following Jesus, the scriptures point to Him! You are wrong, our long-expected Messiah wouldn't die a shameful death! The only book available to them was the Tanakh (the Hebrew Scriptures), from which both sides made their respective cases. One Jewish party claimed continuity, the other postulated radical departure. It is almost painful to observe the mutual acrimony. Instead of just living the Christ-life, the followers of Jesus got themselves into scriptural arguments. Their Master had written nothing (for a good reason) except on the souls of people. It is rather tragic to see that HE became a toy in the hands of scribes.

Paul didn't help the situation much. In his desire to be the super-missionary, he had to be a Jew to the Jews, a Gentile to the Gentiles (1 Corinthians 9:19-23). He mostly preached in the synagogues of the Hellenistic world, where he met genuine Jews, real converts (proselytes), and the "god-fearing", a group of hangers-on, of fence-straddlers, of "seekers" who associated with the synagogue without joining it. His was a balancing act: Yes and No, writing letters about the end of the Law, while affirming it. He was much more of a diplomat than a theologian. It didn't help that he did not exactly have a reputation of having known the "real" Jesus. The Apostles' Council of Jerusalem, AD 50, did not solve the issue of Judaism versus Christianity. It represented a weak compromise (Acts 15). It accepted converts from the Gentile world who were neither circumcised nor adhered to the Judaic dietary laws. The Christian-Jewish wound still lay wide open. We are looking here at a painfully slow process of disassociation where neither side is willing or ready to let go. The Hebrew Scriptures are the holy texts of Jews. A dissident group took and reinterpreted them, especially the prophets and the Book of Psalms. As the first Christian texts were published (letters), step by step, the one text that united and divided them, became an "old" text, the Old Testament, superseded by the New Testament, for ever rubbing in the old grievances: you are "old", i.e. gone, irrelevant; we are "new", up-to-date, pertinent!

What was an inter-Jewish conflict in the beginning changed in nature after Christianity began to be a formative factor within the Roman Empire. The actual Jewish Christian Community in Palestine folded not long after the destruction of the Temple in AD 70. What was left were Pharisees, the one and only branch of Judaism (beside the Sadducees and Essenes) resilient enough to carry on. Probably at a Jewish council at Jamnia, AD 90, the decision was made to excommunicate "Christians" by making it mandatory to pray the birkat haMinim (a curse on Christians) three times daily. Through this excommunication, Judaism regained its identity, orthodoxy, and privileges within the Roman Empire. The ties to the "Jesus-People" were severed, for good.

It is rather ironic that the source of Christian anti-Judaism is Jewish in nature. The Gospel of John and especially the Book of Revelation betray a strong, and now often embarrassing bias. There is much talk here of "the Jews", the "synagogue of Satan", etc., invectives directed at Jews by Jews who were "divided by a common race". Only one major attempt was made to allow Jews to be Jews and Christians to be Christians: Marcion of Sinope was excommunicated in AD 144 for (many objectionable Gnostic theories, rightfully, and) his suggestion that we are dealing here with two fundamentally different religions, ideas, and concepts of God. Although Marcionite churches flourished for over 300 years, in the end the amalgamists won the day: the Old and New Testaments had to stay together, the God of Judaism was identical with the one of Christianity. A major step on the path towards enmity and hatred, pogrom and persecution and expulsion was taken. Christians couldn't help but define themselves in contradistinction to their Jewish brethren. 457 out of 7,959 verses in the New Testament are openly or surreptitiously anti-Judaic. Instead of bearing fruit and so be known as His disciples, the followers of Jesus engaged in futile battles over the correct interpretation of the Hebrew Scriptures. There is much controversy about the Old vs. the New Israel, about circumcision, about dietary laws, Moses, the prophets. None of that has anything to do with the Gospel of Jesus. It side-tracks Christians and insults the intelligence of Jews. Neither the true Gospel nor genuine Judaism can emerge unscathed from this internecine conflict. The often quoted "Judaeo-Christian Culture" is fiction: culture is either Jewish (any good Jew would tell you that much) or Christian, but not both. We need to let go of each other, for the sake of each other.

We are looking back on almost 2,000 years of trying to fit a square peg into a round hole. The church tells us that we need the "Old" Testament for several reasons. One is that we Christians began our journey without a text except the Hebrew one. First generation Christians did not have a "bible" but used the existing one like a quarry from which they mined, with incredible and often irresponsible ingenuity, texts for their missionary purposes. For them, all Christian themes were "foreshadowed" in the old book; there was God's plan hidden in it; prophets spoke of Jesus (without knowing Him); typology and allegory provided the tools to make the Hebrew Scriptures into a Christian book in disguise. The problem is that the "Old Testament" does not say a word about Jesus; its prophets speak to the conditions of their time, they are not clairvoyant predictors of event which are hundreds of years away. They were persecuted and dreaded in their own times because people understood that they they were being addressed, personally, in the Here and Now.

Persecution is not generally meted out to those who speak about possible events hundreds of years down the road. There is no "hidden gospel" in the pages of the Hebrew Scriptures which speak to, well, Hebrews, within their own framework of time and circumstance.

Another reason why we can't seem to let go is our insistence on continuity: whatever is new arises from the old. It is often pointed out that the "Old Testament" is inconclusive, an unfinished work, a book which ends with a question mark or dashes---. It is full of hopes, they say, of prophecies, unfulfilled, unconsummated, in need of the "New Testament" to give it meaning. If the one has the question, the other has the answer; if one ends in darkness and confusion, the other leads to light and knowledge. It is claimed that Jesus cannot be understood except through the eyes of the old prophets. We have the "fulfillment" of "their" hopes and expectations. Any serious Jewish scholar will tell us that we are either seriously deluding ourselves or maliciously encroaching on their territory. Jesus is the Truth, He doesn't have "truths" which can be proven by taking recourse to ancient texts which belong to one people, and to one alone. Even those who understand this are not able to let go: they persist in using the "Old Testament" as a backdrop for the "New Testament" message. We need the old, they say, in order to profile the new. They are the most serious violators of religious peace: they contrast and compare, they present the gospel in stark relief, they herald their "winner" by beating up the "loser".

Of course it is helpful to understand background, places, customs, languages. But Christianity today is as much influenced by Judaism as it is by Platonism or Stoicism (via Paul) or Zoroastrianism/Mazdaism/ Mithraism, or Germanic religion. But we do not include in our Bible the Dialogues of Plato, the Zoroastrian Avesta, or Nordic tales. The Gospel does not become true by comparison, but "eventually": a moment in time when the Word becomes flesh, our flesh and blood, when it "speaks to our condition".

It must become clear by now that we neither need nor want the "Old Testament". It does not belong to us. When we claim that it does, we are prone to distort it. We hijack it from people who are, in most cases, deeply offended by our use of their book. Up until 1979 the Episcopal Church had no readings from the Old Testament on Sundays. For hundreds of years the gospel was proclaimed by reading from the epistles and the gospels only. Historically, the incorporation of the Old Testament into the Christian canon of Biblical books was a massive mistake. Not only did it bind us into a hostile relationship with Jews (who are rightfully displeased) but it betrayed the stand-alone purity of the Gospel the words of which are true in and by themselves, without recourse to secondary buttressing sources.

There are other reasons as well. The mission work of Christianity is seriously hampered by the Old Testament albatross. If the New Testament is the fulfillment of the Old, then new Christians everywhere need to be made aware of this. They must be initiated into the old world to understand the new. They have to become honorary Jews in order to grasp the grace of God in Christ. I do not speak of this problem theoretically. My wife and I were Episcopal missionaries in Africa where, for seven years, we encountered the same issues, over and over again. Here were people with their own cosmogonies, their own ancient lore about the beginning of the world, the root of suffering and evil, their tribal histories of war, domination, misery and redemption. They had their own prophets who spoke of imminent danger and hope. There were mystics who knew what it meant to be claimed by a deity, to speak in other tongues, to be healed by the touch of holy men and women. These people knew religion in a much deeper way than most of us in the West. One anecdote: after a car accident in Dar es Salaam the police officer took down the essentials. He asked me about my first name, last name, address, profession, and then: what tribe? It was in his questionnaire: tribe. There are few more poignant moments in one's life than this one. I was tribe-less, yet I was teaching, at an Anglican Seminary, about the Twelve Tribes, their history; I taught the students Hebrew so they could get closer to those tribes and fully understand the complexities of Christianity. One accident, one question, and it all became clear: we have no business but sharing the Gospel, the pure and unadulterated words of Christ. We are living wrecking balls in the ruins of erstwhile flourishing cultures where "mission" really means occupation, obliteration, imperial control. To bring the Old Testament into non-Christian environments must easily be the most serious crime ever committed in religious history. Old and respected cultures were wiped out, memory was erased and replaced, one great wave of oblivion washed over the minds of the "natives" who, once deracinated, were grafted onto the trunk of a foreign tree. Now it becomes clear that most mission, especially of past centuries, amounts to little more than intellectual rape, a violent conquest of a people, its history, customs, and culture. They may wear Western clothes now, eat baguettes, try their luck at foreign, imposed languages, and apply for scholarships abroad. They received it all, except the Gospel.

In the Name of Jesus I must rise up and protest. Every people under the sun has its own story before Christ. These stories stand as their own "Old Testament". The peoples of the world know God; they have an understanding of creation, of justice and sin, of mercy and forgiveness. They know about spiritual phenomena, about souls, about the After-life. They have their own narratives about the beginning and the end. No one has the right to deprive them of these stories and replace them with the legends of one Middle-Eastern tribe! The Bantu need not cross the Red Sea; the Quechua don't have to eat Manna and quails; the Navajo can leave their boys uncircumcised and eat pork; the Scottish can have their own clans. Nathan Söderblom, Archbishop of the Church of Sweden from 1914 until his death in 1931, saw quite clearly the need for the recognition of all pre-Christian nations. He advocated a kind of mission which would build on existing cultures. "Old Testament": that is the story of every people before it met Christ. Or to be more precise: "Old Testament" is my own story before I met Christ. It includes all my trials and errors, all the futility, all the dead-end streets, all the grievous faults before I saw Him, the Light of the world. This is Gospel. This needs no Hebrew Scriptures, or rather sees them as the legitimate story of the Jewish people before they met Christ. The Old Testament can only be that, "old", to Jews who discover Christ. To the rest of us it is nothing more than an interesting historical document, much as the writings of Greek philosophers or Zoroastrian divines. There are, therefore, many Old Testaments, not just one, all put into perspective, all rendered obsolete by the words of Him who proclaimed, "You have been told from of old.....but I say unto you..." (Mt 5). His words represent a radical departure from all that is old, they offer a completely new vision of God, and man, and salvation. They go far beyond the "old", whatever it was, to open up a new horizon for human existence hitherto unknown to the human race.

There can be waffling no more. We cannot have it both ways. It's either old or new, but not both at the same time. Christian theology must find its way through this thicket and come out on the other side where there is the Way, the Truth, and the Life. The "old" stands for detours, man-made traditions, and living by trial and error. Where Paul and other New Testament writers prevaricate for obvious reasons of making the "gospel" acceptable to all, we can declare our liberty from all law, from all bondage to old texts. We shall no longer wrangle with words, the Word became flesh, and continues to do so in our lives. We shall refuse to be enmeshed in the texts of a book that is not ours, which hampers our spiritual development, and pits us, perpetually, in a war against those among whom Jesus grew up. Enough is enough. Let there be peace, and let it begin with us.

Article VII of the Thirty-Nine Articles (found in the Book of Common Prayer on p. 869) is a prime example of painfully poor theology: *The Old Testament is not contrary to the New: for both in the Old and New Testament everlasting life is offered to Mankind by Christ, who is the only Mediator between God and Man, being both God and Man. Wherefore they are not to be heard, which feign that the old Fathers did look only for transitory promises. Although the Law given from God by Moses, as touching Ceremonies and Rites, do not bind Christian men, nor the Civil precepts thereof ought of necessity to be received in any commonwealth; yet notwithstanding, no Christian man whatsoever is free from the obedience of the Commandments which are called Moral.*

Here it says that the testaments belong together, but that significant parts of the old do not apply. Why that may be so is not explained. It just is. No criterion is mentioned by which we suppress some scriptures and cling to others. It is difficult to understand why a religion which is based on such irrationality and plain ignorance has been able to persist in obscuring the Gospel truth for 2,000 years! It is even more baffling to see that the Revised Common Lectionary doubles or triples the readings from the Old Testament when it is well known that Anglicans have, for hundreds of years, just heard the voice of Christ and His apostles on every Sunday. The homilist will encounter, Sunday after Sunday, the same predicament: how to deal with the scientific problems of the Book of Genesis? How to deal with the moral issues of the books of Exodus to Joshua? How to tweak the message of the prophets into "Christian" ruminations? How to explain the violent and vindictive language of the psalms? Either the sermon will be on the "Old Testament", and then it will not be a Christian sermon in a Christian church. Or it will use the Old Testament texts as a backdrop: this is the way it was, but now..., or: we have come a long ways from those days, thanks be to God! In either case: we are traitors, either to the Gospel of Jesus, or to our professed respect for Jewish brethren and their religion.

Let My People Go: Christians acknowledge the history of all peoples and encourage them to cherish and teach them to their children. They will leave the Hebrew Scriptures to the Hebrews. They will quote them, when necessary, the way they refer to all other historically relevant sources, be they Egyptian, Persian, Greek, or Roman. They will not engage in any discussion about the creation of the world vs Darwin; about prophecies concerning Jesus or the end of the world; or about God's mysterious plan of choosing one nation to bless many. They will read, mark, learn, and inwardly digest the Words of Eternal Life. Where else should we go when HE is the Way?

WORDS OF
ETERNAL LIFE

A Simple Compilation of the Words of Christ, gleaned
from the Christian Bible and extra-Biblical Sources

This selection follows the chronology of the gospels rather
than an ordering principle based on themes or geography.
As words without narrative context they are meant to
speak directly to the reader/listener. I have refrained from
listing the scriptural reference so that the word can stand
on its own. Those who wish to find its place in the Bible
can easily locate it by using a concordance to the Revised
Standard Version. Words of Jesus not found in the gospels
(so-called agrapha) will be marked with an asterisk and a
reference to their provenance.

Man shall not live by bread alone, but by every word that proceeds from the mouth of God.

You shall not tempt the Lord your God.

Begone, Satan! for it is written, `You
shall worship the Lord your God
and him only shall you serve.'

Take these things away; you shall not make
my Father's house a house of trade.

*Become approved moneychangers, rejecting
the [evil] things, and embracing the good.
(Apelles ad Epiph, Haer. XLIV, 2)

Destroy this temple, and in three
days I will raise it up.

Truly, truly, I say to you, unless one is born anew, he cannot see the kingdom of God.

That which is born of the flesh is flesh, and that which is born of the Spirit is spirit.

The wind blows where it wills, and you hear the sound of it, but you do not know whence it comes or whither it goes; so it is with every one who is born of the Spirit.

If I have told you earthly things and you do not believe, how can you believe if I tell you heavenly things?

*I stood in the middle of the world and in flesh I was seen by them. And I found all drunken and I found none thirsty among them. And my soul travails over the sons of men because they are blind in their heart and do not see. (Ox.Pap. 1)

For God so loved the world that he gave his only Son, that whoever believes in him should not perish but have eternal life. For God sent the Son into the world, not to condemn the world, but that the world might be saved through him. He who believes in him is not condemned; he who does not believe is condemned already, because he has not believed in the name of the only Son of God. And this is the judgment, that the light has come into the world, and men loved darkness rather than light, because their deeds were evil. For every one who does evil hates the light, and does not come to the light, lest his deeds should be exposed. But he who does what is true comes to the light, that it may be clearly seen that his deeds have been wrought in God.

The hour is coming, and now is, when the true worshipers will worship the Father in spirit and truth, for such the Father seeks to worship him. God is spirit, and those who worship him must worship in spirit and truth.

My food is to do the will of him who
sent me, and to accomplish his work.

I sent you to reap that for which you
did not labor; others have labored, and
you have entered into their labor.

Unless you see signs and wonders
you will not believe.

The time is fulfilled, and the kingdom of God
is at hand; repent, and believe in the gospel.

Truly, I say to you, no prophet is
acceptable in his own country.

Follow me, and I will make you fishers of men.

*Raise up the stone and there you shall find me. Split the tree and I am there. (Ox.pap. 1)

Let us go on to the next towns, that I may preach there also; for that is why I came out.

I will; be clean.

Take heart, my son; your sins are forgiven.

Those who are well have no need of a physician, but those who are sick. Go and learn what this means, `I desire mercy, and not sacrifice.' For I came not to call the righteous, but sinners.

No one puts a piece of unshrunk cloth on
an old garment, for the patch tears away
from the garment, and a worse tear is made.
Neither is new wine put into old wineskins;
if it is, the skins burst, and the wine is spilled,
and the skins are destroyed; but new wine is put
into fresh wineskins, and so both are preserved.

Do you want to be healed? Take up your
pallet, and walk. See, you are well! Sin no
more, that nothing worse befall you.

Truly, truly, I say to you, he who hears my
word and believes him who sent me, has
eternal life; he does not come into judgment,
but has passed from death to life.

*Jesus, Peace be upon Him, said, The world
is a bridge, so pass over it and do not inhabit
it. (Inscription over main portal of Fateh-
pur-Sikri, India, placed there, in AD 1601,
by the Muslim Grand Mogul Akbar)

I do not receive glory from men. How can you believe, who receive glory from one another and do not seek the glory that comes from the only God?

The sabbath was made for man, not man for the sabbath; so the son of man is lord even of the sabbath.

Blessed are the poor in spirit,
for theirs is the kingdom of heaven.
Blessed are those who mourn,
for they shall be comforted.
Blessed are the meek,
for they shall inherit the earth.
Blessed are those who hunger and thirst for
righteousness, for they shall be satisfied.
Blessed are the merciful,
for they shall obtain mercy.
Blessed are the pure in heart,
for they shall see God.
Blessed are the peacemakers,
for they shall be called sons of God.
Blessed are those who are persecuted
for righteousness' sake,
for theirs is the kingdom of heaven.
Blessed are you when men revile you
and persecute you and utter all kinds
of evil against you falsely on my account.
Rejoice and be glad, for your reward is
great in heaven, for so men persecuted
the prophets who were before you.

You are the salt of the earth; but if salt has lost its taste, how shall its saltness be restored? It is no longer good for anything except to be thrown out and trodden under foot by men.

You are the light of the world. A city set on a hill cannot be hid. Nor do men light a lamp and put it under a bushel, but on a stand, and it gives light to all in the house. Let your light so shine before men, that they may see your good works and give glory to your Father who is in heaven.

Fear not, little flock, for it is your Father's good pleasure to give you the kingdom.

Unless your righteousness exceeds that of the scribes and Pharisees, you will never enter the kingdom of heaven.

You have heard that it was said to the men of old, `You shall not kill; and whoever kills shall be liable to judgment.'
But I say to you that every one who is angry with his brother shall be liable to judgment; whoever insults his brother shall be liable to the council, and whoever says, `You fool!' shall be liable to the hell of fire. So if you are offering your gift at the altar, and there remember that your brother has something against you, leave your gift there before the altar and go; first be reconciled to your brother, and then come and offer your gift.

Make friends quickly with your accuser, while you are going with him to court, lest your accuser hand you over to the judge, and the judge to the guard, and you be put in prison; truly, I say to you, you will never get out till you have paid the last penny.

You have heard that it was said, `You shall not commit adultery.' But I say to you that every one who looks at a woman lustfully has already committed adultery with her in his heart.

If your right eye causes you to sin, pluck it out and throw it away; it is better that you lose one of your members than that your whole body be thrown into hell. And if your right hand causes you to sin, cut it off and throw it away; it is better that you lose one of your members than that your whole body go into hell.

Again you have heard that it was said to the men of old, `You shall not swear falsely, but shall perform to the Lord what you have sworn.' But I say to you, Do not swear at all, either by heaven, for it is the throne of God, or by the earth, for it is his footstool, or by Jerusalem, for it is the city of the great King. And do not swear by your head, for you cannot make one hair white or black. Let what you say be simply `Yes' or `No'; anything more than this comes from evil.

You have heard that it was said, `An eye for an eye and a tooth for a tooth.' But I say to you, Do not resist one who is evil. But if any one strikes you on the right cheek, turn to him the other also; and if any one would sue you and take your coat, let him have your cloak as well; and if any one forces you to go one mile, go with him two miles. Give to him who begs from you, and do not refuse him who would borrow from you.

You have heard that it was said, `You shall love your neighbor and hate your enemy.' But I say to you, Love your enemies and pray for those who persecute you, so that you may be sons of your Father who is in heaven; for he makes his sun rise on the evil and on the good, and sends rain on the just and on the unjust.

For if you love those who love you, what reward have you? Do not even the tax collectors do the same? And if you salute only your brethren, what more are you doing than others? Do not even the Gentiles do the same? You, therefore, must be perfect, as your heavenly Father is perfect.

Beware of practicing your piety before men in order to be seen by them; for then you will have no reward from your Father who is in heaven.

Thus, when you give alms, sound no trumpet before you, as the hypocrites do in the synagogues and in the streets, that they may be praised by men. Truly, I say to you, they have received their reward. But when you give alms, do not let your left hand know what your right hand is doing, so that your alms may be in secret; and your Father who sees in secret will reward you.

And when you pray, you must not be like the hypocrites; for they love to stand and pray in the synagogues and at the street corners, that they may be seen by men. Truly, I say to you, they have received their reward. But when you pray, go into your room and shut the door and pray to your Father who is in secret; and your Father who sees in secret will reward you.

And in praying do not heap up empty phrases as the Gentiles do; for they think that they will be heard for their many words. Do not be like them, for your Father knows what you need before you ask him.

Pray then like this:
Our Father who art in heaven,
Hallowed be thy name.
Thy kingdom come.
Thy will be done,
On earth as it is in heaven.
Give us this day our daily bread;
And forgive us our debts,
As we also have forgiven our debtors;
And lead us not into temptation,
But deliver us from evil.

For if you forgive men their trespasses, your heavenly Father also will forgive you; but if you do not forgive men their trespasses, neither will your Father forgive your trespasses.

And when you fast, do not look dismal, like the
hypocrites, for they disfigure their faces that
their fasting may be seen by men. Truly, I say
to you, they have received their reward. But
when you fast, anoint your head and wash your
face, that your fasting may not be seen by men
but by your Father who is in secret; and your
Father who sees in secret will reward you.

Do not lay up for yourselves treasures on
earth, where moth and rust consume and
where thieves break in and steal, but lay up for
yourselves treasures in heaven, where neither
moth nor rust consumes and where thieves
do not break in and steal. For where your
treasure is, there will your heart be also.

The eye is the lamp of the body. So, if your eye
is sound, your whole body will be full of light;
but if your eye is not sound, your whole body
will be full of darkness. If then the light in
you is darkness, how great is the darkness!

No one can serve two masters; for either he will hate the one and love the other, or he will be devoted to the one and despise the other. You cannot serve God and mammon.

Therefore I tell you, do not be anxious about your life, what you shall eat or what you shall drink, nor about your body, what you shall put on. Is not life more than food, and the body more than clothing?

Look at the birds of the air: they neither sow nor reap nor gather into barns, and yet your heavenly Father feeds them. Are you not of more value than they? And which of you by being anxious can add one cubit to his span of life? And why are you anxious about clothing? Consider the lilies of the field, how they grow; they neither toil nor spin; yet I tell you, even Solomon in all his glory was not arrayed like one of these. But if God so clothes the grass of the field, which today is alive and tomorrow is thrown into the oven, will he not much more clothe you, O men of little faith? Therefore do not be anxious, saying, `What shall we eat?' or `What shall we drink?' or `What shall we wear?' For the Gentiles seek all these things; and your heavenly Father knows that you need them all. But seek first his kingdom and his righteousness, and all these things shall be yours as well. Therefore do not be anxious about tomorrow, for tomorrow will be anxious for itself. Let the day's own trouble be sufficient for the day.

Judge not, that you be not judged. For with the judgment you pronounce you will be judged, and the measure you give will be the measure you get.

Why do you see the speck that is in your brother's eye, but do not notice the log that is in your own eye? Or how can you say to your brother, `Let me take the speck out of your eye,' when there is the log in your own eye? You hypocrite, first take the log out of your own eye, and then you will see clearly to take the speck out of your brother's eye.

Do not give dogs what is holy; and do not throw your pearls before swine, lest they trample them under foot and turn to attack you.

Ask, and it will be given you; seek, and you will find; knock, and it will be opened to you. For every one who asks receives, and he who seeks finds, and to him who knocks it will be opened. Or what man of you, if his son asks him for bread, will give him a stone? Or if he asks for a fish, will give him a serpent? If you then, who are evil, know how to give good gifts to your children, how much more will your Father who is in heaven give good things to those who ask him! So whatever you wish that men would do to you, do so to them; for this is the law and the prophets.

Enter by the narrow gate; for the gate is wide and the way is easy, that leads to destruction, and those who enter by it are many. For the gate is narrow and the way is hard, that leads to life, and those who find it are few.

Beware of false prophets, who come to you in sheep's clothing but inwardly are ravenous wolves.

You will know them by their fruits. Are grapes gathered from thorns, or figs from thistles? So, every sound tree bears good fruit, but the bad tree bears evil fruit. A sound tree cannot bear evil fruit, nor can a bad tree bear good fruit. Every tree that does not bear good fruit is cut down and thrown into the fire. Thus you will know them by their fruits.

Not every one who says to me, `Lord, Lord,' shall enter the kingdom of heaven, but he who does the will of my Father who is in heaven.

Every one then who hears these words of mine and does them will be like a wise man who built his house upon the rock; and the rain fell, and the floods came, and the winds blew and beat upon that house, but it did not fall, because it had been founded on the rock. And every one who hears these words of mine and does not do them will be like a foolish man who built his house upon the sand; and the rain fell, and the floods came, and the winds blew and beat against that house, and it fell; and great was the fall of it.

Blessed is he who takes no offense at me.

Her sins, which are many, are forgiven, for she loved much; but he who is forgiven little, loves little.

And stretching out his hand toward his disciples, he said, "Here are my mother and my brothers! For whoever does the will of my Father in heaven is my brother, and sister, and mother.

Is a lamp brought in to be put under a bushel, or under a bed, and not on a stand?

For there is nothing hid, except to be made manifest; nor is anything secret, except to come to light. If any man has ears to hear, let him hear. Take heed what you hear; the measure you give will be the measure you get, and still more will be given you. For to him who has will more be given; and from him who has not, even what he has will be taken away.

The kingdom of God is as if a man should
scatter seed upon the ground, and should
sleep and rise night and day, and the seed
should sprout and grow, he knows not how.
The earth produces of itself, first the blade,
then the ear, then the full grain in the ear.
But when the grain is ripe, at once he puts
in the sickle, because the harvest has come.

The kingdom of God is not coming with signs
to be observed; nor will they say, `Lo, here
it is!' or `There!' for behold, the kingdom
of God is in the midst of (within) you.

With what can we compare the kingdom of
God, or what parable shall we use for it? It
is like a grain of mustard seed, which, when
sown upon the ground, is the smallest of all the
seeds on earth; yet when it is sown it grows
up and becomes the greatest of all shrubs,
and puts forth large branches, so that the
birds of the air can make nests in its shade.

The kingdom of heaven is like leaven which a woman took and hid in three measures of flour, till it was all leavened.

The kingdom of heaven is like treasure hidden in a field, which a man found and covered up; then in his joy he goes and sells all that he has and buys that field.

Again, the kingdom of heaven is like a merchant in search of fine pearls, who, on finding one pearl of great value, went and sold all that he had and bought it.

Every scribe who has been trained for the kingdom of heaven is like a householder who brings out of his treasure what is new and what is old.

Go home to your friends, and tell them
how much the Lord has done for you,
and how he has had mercy on you.

Daughter, your faith has made you well; go
in peace, and be healed of your disease.

The harvest is plentiful, but the laborers are
few; pray therefore the Lord of the harvest
to send out laborers into his harvest.

And preach as you go, saying, `The kingdom of
heaven is at hand.' Heal the sick, raise the dead,
cleanse lepers, cast out demons. You received
without paying, give without pay. Take no
gold, nor silver, nor copper in your belts, no bag
for your journey, nor two tunics, nor sandals,
nor a staff; for the laborer deserves his food.

Behold, I send you out as sheep in
the midst of wolves; so be wise as
serpents and innocent as doves.

Come away by yourselves to a
lonely place, and rest a while.

Take heart, it is I; have no fear.

*It is more blessed to give than
to receive. (Acts 20:35b)

Do not labor for the food which perishes, but
for the food which endures to eternal life.

It is the spirit that gives life, the flesh
is of no avail; the words that I have
spoken to you are spirit and life.

No one can come to me unless it
is granted him by the Father.

*He that is near me is near the fire.
He that is far from me is far from the
kingdom. (Origen, Latin Homily 20:3)

There is nothing outside a man which by going
into him can defile him; but the things which
come out of a man are what defile him. What
comes out of a man is what defiles a man. For
from within, out of the heart of man, come evil
thoughts, fornication, theft, murder, adultery,
coveting, wickedness, deceit, licentiousness,
envy, slander, pride, foolishness. All these evil
things come from within, and they defile a man.

You know how to interpret the
appearance of the sky, but you cannot
interpret the signs of the times.

Do you not yet perceive or understand?
Are your hearts hardened? Having eyes
do you not see, and having ears do you
not hear? And do you not remember?

Get behind me, Satan! For you are not
on the side of God, but of men.

If any man would come after me, let him deny
himself and take up his cross and follow me.
For whoever would save his life will lose it;
and whoever loses his life for my sake and the
gospel's will save it. For what does it profit a
man, to gain the whole world and forfeit his life?

O faithless generation, how long am I to be
with you? How long am I to bear with you?

All things are possible to him who believes.

If any one would be first, he must
be last of all and servant of all.

Whoever receives one such child in my
name receives me; and whoever receives me,
receives not me but him who sent me.

Whoever causes one of these little ones who
believe in me to sin, it would be better for
him if a great millstone were hung round
his neck and he were thrown into the sea.

Have salt in yourselves, and be at
peace with one another.

Take heed to yourselves; if your brother sins,
rebuke him, and if he repents, forgive him;
and if he sins against you seven times in
the day, and turns to you seven times, and
says, `I repent,' you must forgive him.

As they were going along the road, a man said to him, "I will follow you wherever you go."

And Jesus said to him, "Foxes have holes, and birds of the air have nests; but the Son of man has nowhere to lay his head." To another he said, "Follow me." But he said, "Lord, let me first go and bury my father." But he said to him, "Leave the dead to bury their own dead; but as for you, go and proclaim the kingdom of God." Another said, "I will follow you, Lord; but let me first say farewell to those at my home." Jesus said to him, "No one who puts his hand to the plow and looks back is fit for the kingdom of God."

And when his disciples James and John saw it, they said, "Lord, do you want us to bid fire come down from heaven and consume them?" But he turned and rebuked them, *and He said, "You do not know what manner of spirit you are of; for the Son of man came not to destroy men's lives but to save them." (added by ancient manuscripts)

I thank thee, Father, Lord of heaven and earth, that thou hast hidden these things from the wise and understanding and revealed them to babes; yea, Father, for such was thy gracious will. All things have been delivered to me by my Father; and no one knows the Son except the Father, and no one knows the Father except the Son and any one to whom the Son chooses to reveal him.

Come to me, all who labor and are heavy laden, and I will give you rest. Take my yoke upon you, and learn from me; for I am gentle and lowly in heart, and you will find rest for your souls. For my yoke is easy, and my burden is light.

Blessed are your eyes, for they see, and your ears, for they hear. Truly, I say to you, many prophets and righteous men longed to see what you see, and did not see it, and to hear what you hear, and did not hear it.

Martha, Martha, you are anxious and
troubled about many things; one thing is
needful. Mary has chosen the good portion,
which shall not be taken away from her.

My teaching is not mine, but his who sent me.

Do not judge by appearances, but
judge with right judgment.

Let him who is without sin among you
be the first to throw a stone at her.

If any one thirst, let him come to me and drink.
He who believes in me, as the scripture has said,
`Out of his heart shall flow rivers of living water.

I am the light of the world; he who follows me will
not walk in darkness, but will have the light of life.

You are from below, I am from above; you are
of this world, I am not of this world. I told you
that you would die in your sins, for you will die
in your sins unless you believe that I am he.

*You have dismissed the living one
who is before your eyes and talk idly of
the dead. (Gospel of Thomas, 52)

Truly, truly, I say to you, every one
who commits sin is a slave to sin.

For judgment I came into this world, that
those who do not see may see, and that
those who see may become blind.

I am the good shepherd. The good shepherd
lays down his life for the sheep.

Therefore I tell you, every sin and blasphemy
will be forgiven men, but the blasphemy
against the Spirit will not be forgiven.

Either make the tree good, and its fruit
good; or make the tree bad, and its fruit
bad; for the tree is known by its fruit.

You brood of vipers! how can you speak
good, when you are evil? For out of the
abundance of the heart the mouth speaks.

The good man out of his good treasure
brings forth good, and the evil man out of
his evil treasure brings forth evil. I tell you,
on the day of judgment men will render
account for every careless word they utter;
for by your words you will be justified, and
by your words you will be condemned.

Blessed rather are those who hear
the word of God and keep it!

A disciple is not above his teacher, nor a
servant above his master; it is enough for the
disciple to be like his teacher, and the servant
like his master. If they have called the master
of the house Beelzebul, how much more
will they malign those of his household.

So have no fear of them; for nothing
is covered that will not be revealed, or
hidden that will not be known.

What I tell you in the dark, utter in the light;
and what you hear whispered, proclaim upon
the housetops. And do not fear those who kill
the body but cannot kill the soul; rather fear him
who can destroy both soul and body in hell.

Are not two sparrows sold for a penny? And
not one of them will fall to the ground without
your Father's will. But even the hairs of your
head are all numbered. Fear not, therefore;
you are of more value than many sparrows.

So every one who acknowledges me before
men, I also will acknowledge before my
Father who is in heaven; but whoever
denies me before men, I also will deny
before my Father who is in heaven.

Do not think that I have come to
bring peace on earth; I have not come
to bring peace, but a sword.

Friend, go up higher.

I have come to set a man against his father, and a daughter against her mother, and a daughter-in-law against her mother-in-law; and a man's foes will be those of his own household. He who loves father or mother more than me is not worthy of me; and he who loves son or daughter more than me is not worthy of me; and he who does not take his cross and follow me is not worthy of me. He who finds his life will lose it, and he who loses his life for my sake will find it.

He who receives you receives me, and he who receives me receives him who sent me.

Are not two sparrows sold for a penny? And not one of them will fall to the ground without your Father's will. But even the hairs of your head are all numbered. Fear not, therefore; you are of more value than many sparrows.

Take heed, and beware of all covetousness;
for a man's life does not consist in the
abundance of his possessions. Fool! This
night your soul is required of you; and
the things you have prepared, whose will
they be? So is he who lays up treasure for
himself, and is not rich toward God.

O Jerusalem, Jerusalem, killing the prophets
and stoning those who are sent to you!
How often would I have gathered your
children together as a hen gathers her brood
under her wings, and you would not!

I and the Father are one.

Take heed, watch; for you do not
know when the time will come.

I came to cast fire upon the earth; and would that it were already kindled! I have a baptism to be baptized with; and how I am constrained until it is accomplished! Do you think that I have come to give peace on earth? No, I tell you, but rather division; for henceforth in one house there will be five divided, three against two and two against three; they will be divided, father against son and son against father, mother against daughter and daughter against her mother, mother-in-law against her daughter-in-law and daughter-in-law against her mother-in-law.

Strive to enter by the narrow door; for many, I tell you, will seek to enter and will not be able.

He who loves father or mother more than me is not worthy of me; and he who loves son or daughter more than me is not worthy of me; and he who does not take his cross and follow me is not worthy of me. He who finds his life will lose it, and he who loses his life for my sake will find it.

You are those who justify yourselves
before men, but God knows your hearts;
for what is exalted among men is an
abomination in the sight of God.

When you have done all that is commanded
you, say, `We are unworthy servants; we
have only done what was our duty.'

What therefore God has joined
together, let not man put asunder.

For there are eunuchs who have been so from
birth, and there are eunuchs who have been
made eunuchs by men, and there are eunuchs
who have made themselves eunuchs for the
sake of the kingdom of heaven. He who is
able to receive this, let him receive it.

*Why do you call me good? No
one is good but God alone.*

Let the children come to me, do not hinder
them; for to such belongs the kingdom of God.
Truly, I say to you, whoever does not receive the
kingdom of God like a child shall not enter it.

How hard it will be for those who have riches
to enter the kingdom of God! It is easier for a
camel to go through the eye of a needle than
for a rich man to enter the kingdom of God.

If any one walks in the day, he does not
stumble, because he sees the light of this
world. But if any one walks in the night, he
stumbles, because the light is not in him.

I am the resurrection and the life; he who
believes in me, though he die, yet shall he
live, and whoever lives and believes in me
shall never die. Do you believe this?

You know that those who are supposed to
rule over the Gentiles lord it over them,
and their great men exercise authority over
them. But it shall not be so among you; but
whoever would be great among you must
be your servant, and whoever would be first
among you must be slave of all. For the Son of
man also came not to be served but to serve,
and to give his life as a ransom for many.

You always have the poor with you, and
whenever you will, you can do good to
them; but you will not always have me.

Therefore I tell you, whatever you ask in prayer, believe that you have received it, and it will be yours. And whenever you stand praying, forgive, if you have anything against any one; so that your Father also who is in heaven may forgive you your trespasses.

*Ask for the great things, and God will add unto you the small ones. (Clement of Alexandria, Strom,. I 24, 158)

You are not to be called rabbi, for you have one teacher, and you are all brethren. And call no man your father on earth, for you have one Father, who is in heaven. Neither be called masters, for you have one master, the Christ. He who is greatest among you shall be your servant; whoever exalts himself will be humbled, and whoever humbles himself will be exalted.

Heaven and earth will pass away, but my words will not pass away.

Truly, I say to you, as you did it to one of the least of these my brethren, you did it to me.

What I am doing you do not know now, but afterward you will understand.

Take; this is my body. This is my blood of the covenant, which is poured out for many.

A new commandment I give to you, that you love one another; even as I have loved you, that you also love one another. By this all men will know that you are my disciples, if you have love for one another.

As the Father has loved me, so have I loved you; abide in my love. Greater love has no man than this, that a man lay down his life for his friends.

I do not pray for these only, but also for those
who believe in me through their word, that they
may all be one; even as thou, Father, art in me,
and I in thee, that they also may be in us, so that
the world may believe that thou hast sent me.

Abba, Father, all things are possible to
thee; remove this cup from me; yet not
what I will, but what thou wilt.

Would you betray the Son of man with a kiss?

Daughters of Jerusalem, do not weep for me,
but weep for yourselves and for your children.

My God, my God, why hast thou forsaken me?

Father, into thy hands I commit my spirit!

It is finished.

Receive the Holy Spirit. If you forgive the sins of any, they are forgiven; if you retain the sins of any, they are retained.

Do not be faithless, but believing.

All authority in heaven and on earth has been given to me. Go therefore and make disciples of all nations, baptizing them in the name of the Father and of the Son and of the Holy Spirit, teaching them to observe all that I have commanded you; and lo, I am with you always, to the close of the age.